The Bitcoin Book

Simplifying Bitcoin so you can Thrive in the New

Digital Economy

By Josh Miller and Matt Lopez

To learn more, click or visit:
www.cryptomavericks.io

Special Bonus Offer:

Our mission is the put the power of blockchain technology into the hands of billions of people. One of the ways we accomplish this mission the through education. As a reader of this book, we'd like to offer you some exclusive content that is not in this book.

Follow the link below to sign up for our mailing list and as a special thank you, we'll give you a Free guide that tells you everything you need to know about securing your cryptocurrency so your funds are NEVER lost or stolen.

Link: http://security.cryptomavericks.io/freeguide

Table of Contents

Chapter 1: What the Heck Is Bitcoin?..........................11

Chapter 2: Why Is Bitcoin a Revolutionary
Technology 26

    Bitcoin's Properties Beat Gold and Fiat 32

    Censorship Resistant 33

    Sound Money..37

    Trustless, Private, and Secure 47

    Faster and More Cost-Effective Way of
    Transferring Money...51

    The Bitcoin Effect...54

Chapter 3: How to Use Bitcoin 61

    Wallets and Exchanges...62

    Public and Private Keys...66

    Before You Buy...75

    Buying Bitcoin 81

    Safely Storing Your Bitcoin....................................85

    Spending Bitcoin..89

    Accepting Bitcoin as a Business 90

About the Authors..98

References 100

Introduction

The year was 2012. I was still in high school at the time. I've always read a lot about finance and technology from a young age. As soon as I heard about bitcoin in the spring of that year, I was immediately intrigued.

I have to admit, I got pretty deep into it. I read and watched everything I could on the subject. I would stay up until 4:00 and 5:00 in the morning just devouring it. It didn't take me long after that to buy my first bitcoin.

Buying bitcoin back then wasn't like it is now. I had to use some sketchy exchanges, one of which was Mt. Gox. I made a big mistake: I left my bitcoin on the exchange and lost more than 40 bitcoins because of it. (At the peak that was worth over $700,000!)
Ouch!! That hurt.
That was my first lesson in crypto: Don't leave your coins on the exchange!!

You see, crypto is about putting the power in the hands of the people. It was this mission to empower people financially that made me so passionate about bitcoin in the first place. But as it's been said, "With great power comes great responsibility." Losing forty bitcoins showed me how important it was that I educate people on how to safely use this technology. It's that combination of the mission and the lessons I've learned over the past six years in crypto that led me to write this book.

I've written this book with my longtime friend and business partner, Matt Lopez. I tried to get him into bitcoin back in 2013, but like many people, he was skeptical. It wasn't until 2016 that the flip switched for him and he became deeply involved alongside me.

Together, we have a total of almost ten years of experience in the industry, and we've done just about everything you can think of. From day-trading to investing in cryptocurrency startups, running nodes, mining, using dApps, building blockchain startups, coding smart contracts … The list goes on and on. You name it, we've done it.

Throughout the last six years, we've learned how to safely and successfully navigate the crypto industry. We've uncovered all the "hidden secrets." We've used all the tools and resources. We've taken the time to understand how this whole industry works so we can better explain it to you. We've spent countless hours and many late nights studying everything we can about this technology, learning it inside and out. Our goal in this book is to distill the most important information about bitcoin into one simple, easy-to-read text that makes it so anyone can understand.

Most importantly, we've learned that to do anything well in this industry, you must have integrity. We've seen many get-rich-quick schemes, pump-and-dump ICOs, and shady businesses built around crypto. While there's nothing wrong with wanting to make money, we've decided that our mission is to educate people, first and foremost.

Bitcoin and cryptocurrencies can seem like a complicated and mysterious concept. People often view them as some kind of magic internet money that doesn't exist in the real world.

That's normal for any new technological innovation. If I had tried to explain to you how email or the internet worked in 1990, you would have looked at me with a confused face. But today, we use these technologies on a daily basis without thinking twice about how they work, it's just second nature to us.

The same is true for bitcoin. After my first few months of using bitcoin, it felt as natural to me as using regular dollars. Cryptocurrencies are not nearly as difficult to use and understand as they seem. That being said, there are many nuances and things you need to be aware of before you dive head in.

One word you will hear a lot in the same sentence as bitcoin is "blockchain." The blockchain is the underlying technology that supports bitcoin. You can think of blockchain as the road, while bitcoin is the car. This is also similar to the way the internet is the infrastructure that supports all the applications we use today. Without the internet, you wouldn't be able to use Facebook, WhatsApp, Uber, or any other app on your computer or mobile phone. The blockchain is to bitcoin what the internet is to Facebook. Bitcoin was the first application built on the blockchain, but certainly not the last.

The blockchain is widely accepted to be a revolutionary technology capable of decentralizing many traditional business practices. However, you don't need to understand the blockchain to use bitcoin and other cryptocurrencies. Again, we use the internet on a daily basis yet most of us have no idea what's going on behind the scenes that makes it work the way it does. When we type in "Facebook.com" into our browser, all we see is the social networking website that pops up.

The same goes for blockchain. As an everyday user of bitcoin, we don't really get to *see* the blockchain at all. With the internet, we don't get to see the packets of data that are routed through a default gateway and translated through a Domain Name Server. All we see are the websites and apps on our phone. With the bitcoin and the blockchain, we don't get to see all of the intricacies that go into the system to make it happen, all we see are wallets, exchanges, and public addresses. (We'll get into all of these concepts in detail in the book.)

Bitcoin may seem like a foreign subject to you right now, but it's important to keep in mind that it's not nearly as confusing as it's made out to be.
Bitcoin is simply a way of sending money from one person to another without the need for banks and a middleman.

It is supposed to make sending money simpler, not more complex. Thankfully, that's exactly what it does.

Chapter 1

What Is Bitcoin and How Does it Work?

> Bitcoin is an easy, cost-effective to send money to anyone anywhere in the world without the need for banks and middlemen.
>
> —Josh Miller

While bitcoin is an amazing invention in its own right, it was not the first attempt to create a digital currency. In 1998, a man named Nick Szabo came up with an idea called "bitgold." Bitgold is the closest precursor to bitcoin you can find. Like bitcoin, it was an attempt to create a decentralized digital currency.

However, it wasn't until January 9, 2009, that bitcoin was officially released to the world. While the real person or group behind the bitcoin still remains unknown, they used "Satoshi Nakamoto" as a pseudonym. Along with the release of bitcoin also came a whitepaper detailing how it worked, referring to bitcoin as a "peer-to-peer electronic cash system."

You might be thinking, *"Okay, so I get that Satoshi invented Bitcoin, but who runs it today?"*
Here's where it gets interesting: Nobody runs bitcoin.

If you've been on Wikipedia before, you know that it's a free online encyclopedia where anyone can become an editor. If you wanted to, you could go onto Wikipedia right now and create a page or edit an existing one. Wikipedia is moderated by the community. If someone thinks a member of the community is spamming or editing inappropriately, they will flag that content and have it removed from the site. This way, the power is distributed amongst the members of the community and not held by one authority. It would not be possible for one party to control Wikipedia.

Bitcoin works in a similar manner. Just as anyone can join the Wikipedia community, anyone can join the bitcoin network. Like Wikipedia, the power in the bitcoin network is distributed amongst the community. Individuals and groups can gain more of an influence in certain ways, but they can never fully control bitcoin or Wikipedia.

Neither bitcoin nor Wikipedia are corporations, rather, they are tools and technologies that were created to put the power in the hands of the users. Wikipedia was designed to be an unbiased source of information. Bitcoin was designed to be an unbiased form of money.

Early Adoption

Bitcoin was released after the 2008 financial crisis at a time when some people felt betrayed by the current financial system in the United States. Many of the early supporters came from a very strong libertarian and anarcho-capitalist background. These are people who disagree with idea of big governments intervening in their personal business and finances. They blamed the banks and governments on the financial crisis and viewed bitcoin as an alternative to the current banking system. Bitcoin also had a large support from a group referred to as "cypherpunks." These are people who try to maintain their privacy on the internet through the use of various technologies. Bitcoin, being that it is relatively anonymous, was a perfect fit for this crowd as well.

The first product-market fit for bitcoin was with the dark market. The dark market is an online marketplace where anything can be bought and sold, often times drugs and counterfeit goods. This would turn out to be a bit of a black eye in the face of bitcoin. People would begin to associate it with drugs and illegal activities. However, the criminal underground world was so important to bitcoin's early development that it's quite possible it would never have become what it is today without them. And while it is true bitcoin is still used for illegal purposes, it has since become much more accepted in society as currency with a real use-case other than just hiding from authorities.

How Bitcoin Works (A Simple Explination)

The number one component that makes bitcoin so unique is this thing called "proof-of-work". This sounds complex, but it's simply just a way of making sure that the same bitcoin cannot be spent twice.

What it entails is a process where these computers called "miners" use their computing power to solve math problems to verify that each transaction has been worked on and is valid.

Here's an analogy that should help it make sense:

Let's say you're in math class. At the beginning of class, your teacher gives you and the rest of the class a math problem to solve. Everyone has ten minutes to solve the problem.

The first person to answer the question correctly receives extra credit for the class. To receive the extra credit, they also have to show all of their work on how they got their answer. Any student who arrived at the right answer but did not show their work will not receive credit.

If a student shows their work but it does not match up with how the problem is supposed to be formatted, they will not receive any credit either.

In other words, the final answer *and* all of the work must be correct for the student to receive the extra credit.

The teacher has already solved the problem herself. Her answer is on a covered sheet of paper on her desk. The students can all see that it's there, but they cannot what see the answer is. The teacher then writes the question on the board and starts the timer for the students to begin their work. As each student completes the problem, they turn their paper in to the teacher so she knows who finished first. After ten minutes is up, the teacher collects all the remaining papers and begins grading them.

After the grading is done, the teacher reveals the work of the student who got the correct answer. She also reveals her answer so the students can see that the two answers match up. This way, everyone knows she's not playing favorites with one of the students. It is provably fair that the student who received the extra credit was, in fact, the one who got the problem correct.

Once the answers are revealed to the students, the teacher asks everyone to sign off and say that it was fair. The entire class approves, and they can move on with their day.

This is very similar conceptually to how bitcoin transactions work as well. Instead of extra credit, we are dealing with the transfer of digital money. The students solving these problems are called "miners" on the bitcoin network. Just like the students, these miners are solving complex math problems. The first miner to come up with the right answer receives a reward in the form of bitcoin.

What the miners are in effect doing is two things:

1. They are processing the transaction so money can be sent from one person to the other.
2. They are proving to everyone that the bitcoin cannot be double spent and the transaction is valid.

Just like in the math class, each bitcoin transaction has been worked on and solved by one miner and validated by all of the other participants. This way, everyone on the network knows that each transaction is valid.

The miners receive a reward in the form of bitcoin, so they are happy. The people sending and receiving bitcoin can now send money without having to trust the other side or a third party, so they are happy. It's a win-win for everyone.

The system is designed to make it extremely hard for

someone to cheat. If one student wanted to try to sabotage the others by saying the extra credit assignment was unfair, the other student would be able to override this decision with majority rule. If a group of students wanted to gang up together and try, they would need to have 51 percent of the students on their side. In a classroom environment, this might be possible, but with hundreds of thousands of computers on the bitcoin network, it's not.

By now you might notice a trend in what's going on here. What this whole system is about is this idea of achieving a "decentralized consensus". Or in other words, a system where a large amount of people can come to an agreement about something that's beneficial for everyone. When power is distributed, no one can exploit it for their personal benefit, everyone has to play by the rules. Wikipedia has done a very effective job at accomplishing this. In a way, what bitcoin has done is taken what Wikipedia has and applied a business model to it where you can be financially rewarded for keeping the system in check. With Wikipedia, editors contribute out of the goodness of their heart. With bitcoin, you can contribute and be compensated for it.

Why Is This a Big Deal?

Again, proof of work is a big deal because it solves something called the "Byzantine Generals Problem" also known as the "double-spend problem." This is a problem where you can double spend currency. The internet we use today does not allow us to create unique digital assets. If I texted or emailed you a picture, how would you know I didn't keep a copy for myself or send it to other people? This is the reason piracy is a problem. Proof of work eliminates this sort of problem by using miners to verify transactions. This is a big deal because it means for the first time in history we can transfer money directly from one person to another without needing to trust someone else.

But the proof of work consensus is not the only factor that makes bitcoin so unique. There are some additional factors listed below that all work with one another to allow bitcoin to function the way it does.

- **Decentralized (aka Peer-to-Peer network).**

A peer-to-peer network is one in which individual computers join to form the network rather than having servers that are controlled by one central party. In a peer-to-peer, there is no center of authority. This goes hand in hand with proof of work to eliminate the need for middlemen.

The way bitcoin is decentralized is not much different than Napster or BitTorrent. You may remember Napster if you were listening to music in the 2000s. It was a peer-to-peer file-sharing technology that eventually got shut down. What it showed us, though, was the power of sharing information directly from one person to another.

In bitcoin, a "peer" is often referred to as a "node." Each node holds a copy of the bitcoin ledger. Miners are one example of a node, but you don't have to mine to be a node. Anyone can join the network and become a node. Being a node is similar to being an editor on Wikipedia; you are now part of the community and have certain privileges.

- **Transparent and Immutable Ledger.** Bitcoin's

ledger is also an extremely important component to how the whole system works. The "transparent" part means all of the transactions are recorded on an open ledger for anyone to see. If you know someone's public address, you can see their entire transaction history. As you might imagine, this is what makes bitcoin and the blockchain so transparent. This is an advantage because, since everyone can see what's going on, no one can get away with lying about it.

The "immutable" part means no one can go back and change the data once it's been recorded onto the blockchain. This is unlike traditional databases where someone can easily make changes. After each transaction is processed by the miners, it is added to the blockchain. Each transaction is time stamped an all of the nodes receive an updated copy of the ledger.

You can think of the ledger like one giant shared Google Docs. Everyone on the bitcoin network can see this Google Docs, and changes are updated in real time. But again, unlike a Google

Docs, the bitcoin ledger is immutable. For that reason, it would be more like a Google Docs that anyone can view and add to, but not go back and make changes to previous work that's been done.

- **Digital.** Bitcoin has often been referred to as "digital gold." Since bitcoin exists only in a digital format, it has made it much easier to transact than gold. The ledger that we mentioned above is also completely digital. This could mean a significant reduction in costs for businesses and governments.

- **Open Source.** The code to bitcoin is open source. This means that anyone can see how bitcoin works and even build their own version of it. When a project is open source, it also tends to mean it's more transparent. In the math class example mentioned earlier, when the teacher reveals her answer to the class, she is in effect open-sourcing the code to the math problem.

- **Limited Supply.** The total number of bitcoins that can ever be in existence is limited to 21 million. It's estimated that all 21 million will have been mined sometime around 2140.

- **Pseudonymous.** Some people mistakenly think that bitcoin is anonymous when, in fact, it is pseudonymous. Every transaction that you send will have a public address attached to it. That transaction will then be recorded on an open ledger for everyone to see. When you send bitcoin, everyone in the world can see that money was just transferred. The part that makes it pseudonymous is that there's no personal information associated with each transaction. Everyone can see that money was just transferred, but they can't see who sent it or who it was transferred to. All they can see is the amount that was sent and the public addresses of the two parties. You don't need to give up your name or email to obtain a public address. Here is a quote from Satoshi himself on the subject:

  The possibility to be anonymous or pseudonymous relies on you not revealing any identifying information about yourself in connection with the bitcoin addresses you use. If you post your bitcoin address on the web, then you're associating that address and any transactions with it with the name you posted under. For greater privacy, it's best to use bitcoin addresses only once.[i]

So now you know the basics of what bitcoin is and how it works, but to really solidify it, let's walk through a bitcoin transaction from start to finish. Let's say Bob want to send some bitcoin to Alice, here's how it would go:

1. Bob begins the transaction by copying and pasting Alice's public address or scanning her QR code.
2. Once Bob hits "send," the transaction is broadcasted to the network for the miners to begin working on.

3. The miners are trying to solve computer problems to prove the transaction is valid. The first miner to solve it gets a reward in bitcoin.

4. After the first miner finds the answer, it has to be approved by the other peers on the network. (It usually takes 3 confirmations.)

5. Once the transaction is approved by the other peers, it is recorded onto the blockchain.

6. Alice now sees that the transaction has been confirmed, and she receives her bitcoin from Bob.

Chapter 2

Why Bitcoin is a Revolutionary Technology

> I do think Bitcoin is the first [encrypted money] that has the potential to do something like change the world.
>
> —Peter Thiel

Now you know what bitcoin is and the basics of how it works, but what makes it so important? We can't just say, *"Use bitcoin because I say so."* I will admit there is something inherently cool about bitcoin. However, the coolness factor will only take it so far. For it to gain any kind of mass adoption, there have to be some real-world use cases that make bitcoin a compelling currency for people to use.

When most people think about what money is, they immediately think of fiat currency. Fiat currency is a form of money that is issued and controlled by governments.

It's not backed by anything except faith in the government that issued it. Most countries around the world today use fiat currency. It's the paper money in your wallet right now.

But fiat currency is not perfect. There are some weaknesses with fiat currencies that make bitcoin a compelling option.

For anything to be considered "money," it must serve three basic functions:

1. **Medium of Exchange**. You must be able to use it to transact and pay for the goods and services you consume.
2. **Unit of Account**. You must be able to use it to easily measure the cost of the goods and services you consume.
3. **Store of Value**. You must be able to store it and have it maintain its value over time.

Medium of Exchange

Bitcoin works great as a medium of exchange because of how easy it is to send and receive. Transactions on the bitcoin network are fast, reliable, and nearly frictionless.

The only problem with sending bitcoin to someone is that they may not want to accept it.

Dollars are still preferred over bitcoin by most people since the price of bitcoin will fluctuate on a daily basis. A merchant won't want to accept bitcoin and have it lose 10 percent of its market value the next day. What this means is there needs to be a quick and easy way to exchange bitcoin for dollars without any price risk. Thankfully, there is.

There are a few companies that allow you to hold bitcoin on an account that is linked to a debit card. When you are ready to spend the bitcoin, you just swipe the card and it instantly converts to cash to pay for your items. The seller won't even know you've just paid in bitcoin. All they see is the cash in their account.

On the seller side, accepting bitcoin as a business is as easy as setting up a payment gateway with any traditional service. (We'll cover how to accept bitcoin as a business in a later chapter)

As time goes on, it's likely that bitcoin will only become a better medium of exchange for two main reasons.

The first reason is that as bitcoin becomes more mainstream, more businesses will feel comfortable accepting it as payment. As more people use bitcoin as a currency, the price will become more stable which would further incentivize people to use it as a currency rather than just speculating on the price.

The second reason is that the technology for bitcoin will continue to improve making it an even easier and faster way of sending money.

Store of Value

It's also likely that bitcoin will prove to be a better store of value than fiat currency. This is because, unlike fiat currency, bitcoin is truly scarce. There will only ever be 21 million bitcoins in existence. This means that bitcoin is "sound money," which we'll talk in depth about in just a minute.

As long as bitcoin continues to be an efficient way of transferring money, people will continue to use it. If people continue to use it, it will maintain some value. We don't know exactly what that value will be. What we do know is that when there is a limited supply and a continuous demand, prices go up. This is why people will make crazy high predictions about the future price of bitcoin. I'm not going to make a price prediction myself, but I can see how some of these people arrive at such high numbers. If bitcoin were able to take just 10 percent of the market share of gold, it would put the price per bitcoin at around $40,000. I'm not saying it will be easy for bitcoin to take market share from gold, but it's not hard for me to imagine either.

Another thing to mention is that being a store of value and a medium of exchange are not mutually exclusive. For something to be a good medium of exchange, it must also be a good store of value. The reason why people accept dollars is because they know they can use them in the future. If you thought your dollars would become worthless tomorrow, you wouldn't want to accept them. As bitcoin becomes a better medium of exchange, it will also help its case as a store of value, and vice versa.

Do keep in mind that bitcoin is still far from being a "proven" store of value the way gold and real estate are. It has come a long way since 2009, but it will still have to prove itself in many ways for it to be considered a true store of value.

Unit of Account

The unit of accounts is a bit of a hurdle for bitcoin.

US dollars make a good unit of account because the value of the dollar is held relatively stable. You know that a dollar received today will be worth about the same amount a year from now. This is why everything we value, including bitcoin, is measured in dollars.

Because bitcoin is so scarce, the price per bitcoin has become very high. Bitcoin is divisible to eight decimal places, making it so that you can own 0.00000001 bitcoin.

Overall, this is an advantage, but it makes it confusing for people when they see that something costs 0.00172 bitcoins. It's not exactly easy to measure the costs of items with bitcoin.

To add to that, there's also a lot of speculation and trading going on, which can result in wild price swings. It's confusing when something costs 0.00172 bitcoins, but when all of a sudden it costs 0.0025 bitcoins instead, that makes it way more confusing.

Bitcoin's Properties Beat Gold and Fiat

In addition to fulfilling the three roles mentioned above, money should also have the following properties:

- **Fungible**: One unit can be exchanged for another.
- **Portable**: Can take it with you where you go.
- **Durable**: Able to withstand repeated use.
- **Divisible**: Can be divided into smaller units.
- **Scarce**: Can only be so many in existence.

When we look at how bitcoin compares to gold and fiat currency, it has better properties in almost every category:

- It's easily fungible because you can trade one bitcoin for another.
- It is far more portable than gold.
- It is far more durable than fiat currency.
- It is easily divisible, unlike gold.
- It has true scarcity, unlike fiat currency which governments can just print more of.

Censorship Resistant

Power tends to corrupt;
absolute power corrupts
absolutely.

—Lord Acton

When something is censorship resistant, it means that no central or third party can have complete control over it. You may have noticed that Facebook, for example, is censored. The same goes for YouTube and almost all of the other social networks on the internet today. When you upload a video to YouTube or post something to Facebook, you no longer own that content. YouTube or Facebook can choose to delete it—not because it was illegal or anything, but just because they didn't like it.

The same is true with banks and money. When you deposit your money at a bank, you are no longer in full control over it. You are a creditor to the bank, and they decide who you can send your money to. Just like Facebook, if a bank doesn't like who you're sending

JOSH MILLER AND MATT LOPEZ

money to, they can flag it as suspicious and freeze your account.

For most law-abiding citizens in developed countries, this isn't as much of an issue. But take Cuba, for instance. When Fidel Castro took power, one of the first things he did was take complete control of the banks so no one could withdraw their funds. Cubans were forced to leave behind their life savings in bank accounts controlled by Fidel.

Cuba is not the only country to have imposed strict banking controls over their citizens. Cyprus did the same thing when their banks made loans to Greece that went bad. The government declared a banking holiday and prevented people from withdrawing their funds. Remember that ledger we talked about in chapter one? With the banking systems that exist today, that ledger is controlled by one central party. Governments, banks, and financial institutions are all able to change the amount of money in your bank account simply by making changes to the ledger.

PayPal, for instance, has one ledger that stores all of the data that determines who owns what. If PayPal wanted to, they could take all the money out of anyone's account or freeze their funds at any time. And sometimes, they do. PayPal is also at the mercy of governments that can strong-arm them into doing what they want.

If you jaywalk in Shanghai, China, there are cameras with facial recognition that will detect who you are, then instantly withdraw money from your WeChat account without your consent. Even the US government has taken money from innocent people's bank accounts when they didn't like what they were doing.[ii]

This is why there is a need for bitcoin.

As Nassim Nicholas Taleb puts it:

> Bitcoin is an excellent idea. It fulfills the needs of the complex system, not because it is a cryptocurrency, but precisely because it has no owner, no authority that can decide on its fate. It is owned by the crowd, its users. And it now has a track record of several years, enough for it to be an animal in its own right.[iii]

What makes bitcoin so empowering is that it doesn't have one centralized ledger controlled by one party. Instead, the ledger is stored as a copy on over 100,000 computers spread across the globe that no one party can control. This is what makes bitcoin "decentralized."

What this means for you and I is that when we own bitcoin, we are in complete control over our money. We can send bitcoin to whoever we want anywhere in the world at any time.

Owning bitcoin is somewhat similar to having an offshore bank account, the difference being that a bitcoin wallet is a thousand times easier to set up and is accessible to everyone, not just the ultra-rich. The reason why so many wealthy people have offshore bank accounts is so they're not at the mercy of one government that can confiscate their funds.

However, there is a cost to this. When you own bitcoin, there is no one holding your money for you. What this means is that if you lose your bitcoin, it's gone forever. Bitcoin is extremely empowering, but there is also more liability involved. "With great power comes great responsibility." You have to be especially careful in securing your bitcoin so you don't lose it and no one can steal it from you.

Sound Money

Bitcoin is limited to how many bitcoins can ever be produced, unlike [fiat] currency that governments can just create as many more of as they ever wanted to.

—Steve Wozniak

Most banks around the world operate on what's called a "fractional reserve" banking system. This means that banks only have to keep a fraction of what you deposit on hand ready for you to pick up. In the United States, the reserve requirement is about 10 percent. The other 90 percent of the money you deposited is lent out so the bank can earn interest and make a profit.

This system works as long as everyone has faith in the banks. But when banks make bad loans (as they did in

2008), it's everyday people who get hit the hardest.

You might think, *Well, thankfully, the government bailed out the banks, and everything is okay.*
Not quite.

The government bailed out the banks to prevent what would have been a global financial meltdown. As a result, all of the bailout money, artificially low interest rates, and quantitative easing will cause inflation in the long run.

Inflation is defined as the rise in prices for goods and services in an economy, but you can also think about it as the devaluing of a currency. Businesses have to raise their prices because the dollars they're being paid with are becoming worth less overtime. Printing money has a positive correlation with inflation. The more governments print money, the more inflation there will be. The more inflation there is, the lower the value of the currency will become.

As a simple way of remembering this relationship, when you see the word "inflation," imagine a balloon. In that balloon is the total supply of money in an economy. When the government increases the money supply, they are inflating the balloon. By inflating the balloon, they are also inflating the prices of goods and services in the economy. If the United States decided to give out $1 million to every household, everyone would feel a lot richer—until they realized their currency had become devalued and everything they need to buy is now much more expensive.

This is because when you increase the supply of something, you decrease the value or cost of that item per unit. This sounds complicated when we talk about it in terms of economics, but it's a concept your already familiar with. If there are only ten of a specific Babe Ruth baseball card in the world, each one would be worth a lot more than if there were ten million of them. Since the Babe Ruth baseball card is rare and the supply is limited, each one is a lot more valuable.

When the Federal Reserve increases the money supply, they increase the amount of money there is to be lent out. And as you now know, a greater the supply of something the lower the cost per unit will be. The increase in the supply of money to be lent out decreases the cost of borrowing the money, otherwise known as "interest rates."

The lower interest rates will make it more attractive for businesses and individuals to borrow money and use credit. This means more people buying houses, taking out car loans, business loans, and buying consumer goods. The lower interest increases demand for goods and services. This increase in demand will then increase the prices for those goods and services. Now, the same $3 carton of milk you used to buy will cost you $3.30.

In a nutshell, this is how inflation works.

Governments create inflation by printing money and lowering interest rates. This makes the dollars you own worth less overtime, and the goods and services you consume more expensive. Governments print money when they need to boost the economy, and they contract the money supply when there is too much inflation. This creates a boom-and-bust cycle where we have an expansion in the economy followed by a recession or correction. However, this boom-and-bust cycle is not the problem. The problem is when governments print too much money and end up creating an unsustainable amount of inflation.

As governments increase in size, they take on more debt. As they take on more debt, their ability to pay back their debt decreases and they end up either having to increase taxes or print more money to compensate. If they choose to print money, it will result in higher inflation and a more unstable economic condition altogether.

> The U.S. government has a technology, called a printing press (or today, its electronic equivalent), that allows it to produce as many U.S. dollars as it wishes at no cost.
>
> —Ben Bernanke, former chairman of the US Federal Reserve.[iv]

Every fiat currency has failed at some point. The average life expectancy for a fiat currency is about twenty-seven years. Gold, on the other hand, has been used as currency since around 700 BC. Gold is a good example of "sound" money.

Sound money is a form of money where the purchasing power is determined by the supply-and-demand forces of the market. Unlike fiat currency, sound money is independent of governments and political parties. Sound money must be inherently scarce and cannot be inflated like fiat currency. Sound money also can't be controlled by a central party.

No one controls bitcoin, the same way no one controls gold. Bitcoin is also an example of sound money because of how it is both decentralized and scarce. As you already know, bitcoin is censorship resistant. There is no central party that sets the price of bitcoin. The rate of inflation, which is relatively small, is predetermined and transparent for everyone to see. And as time goes on, it becomes harder to mine new bitcoins and the rate of inflation will steadily decline.

> As computers get faster and the total computing power applied to creating bitcoins increases, the difficulty increases proportionally to keep the total new production constant. Thus, it is

known in advance how many new bitcoins will be created every year in the future.

—Satoshi[v]

There have been some good jokes made about the wild price swings of bitcoin.

One of my favorites goes like this:
A boy asks his dad for one bitcoin for his birthday. His dad says, "What? $15,554?! $14,354 is a lot of money! What do you need $16,782 for anyway?"

The volatility of bitcoin is largely because most people are still speculating on its price movements.
But even in spite of the volatility, bitcoin is a far better currency than a fiat currency with hyperinflation. Take Venezuela, for example, a country that has suffered from tremendous hyperinflation. What bitcoin has done for Venezuelans is given the people a currency they can use and trust. With bitcoin, Venezuelans have been able to trade it to make money, mine it to pay their rent, use it to buy food, and even escape the country with it.[vi]

There are many other countries around the world that would also benefit from adopting bitcoin. It's not just billionaires like Peter Thiel and Jack Dorsey who will benefit from using bitcoin as a store of value; it's everyday people who are hurt the most by inflation. Wealthier people are more invested in the stock market. When central banks create inflation, a byproduct of that inflation is often a rise in stock prices. Poorer people don't get to see their wealth appreciate, because they're not nearly as invested. Poorer people also spend a greater percentage of their income on goods and services that increase in price with inflation. If rent increases 5 percent year after year, this will disproportionately affect poorer people.

What's great about bitcoin it has the potential democratize wealth by providing a store of value that is not inflated and restricted by governments. Bitcoin also makes it easy for anyone to participate, however, people will still need to invest to reap the benefits.

In addition to bitcoin, what the blockchain is doing is creating its own free-market economy. There are many startups emerging now that are using the blockchain to increase transparency and remove costly middlemen. This could mean lower interest rates for borrowers, higher returns for lenders, more accurate price discovery, and much more.

With the blockchain, everything is transparent and based on supply and demand. Governments obscure pricing for goods with subsidies, taxes incentives, and government programs. This could mean you might pay less for something up front, but more for it with taxes or inflation later on. This also means that money is being diverted away from efficient areas in an economy into less efficient ones.

Bitcoin and blockchain will not only be a trusted currency to countries like Venezuela, but also a force for creating a global free-market economy. We will not have to have central banks and governments inflate our money supply and devalue our currency.

> The root problem with conventional currency is all the trust that's required to make it work. The central bank must be trusted not to debase the currency, but

the history of fiat currencies is full of breaches of that trust. Banks must be trusted to hold our money and transfer it electronically, but they lend it out in waves of credit bubbles with barely a fraction in reserve. We have to trust them with our privacy, trust them not to let identity thieves drain our accounts.

— Satoshi Nakamoto, [vii]

Let me be clear, though: I am not saying you should ditch your fiat currency and start living off bitcoin. Unless you like in a country like Venezuela, that would not be a wise idea.

What I *am* saying, though, is that having some exposure to an asset class that is not correlated to what federal governments and central banks are doing could be a good idea. Bitcoin could prove to be the perfect hedge against big governments and inflation. But of course, talk to a financial advisor before making any investment decisions.

Trustless, Private, and Secure

Another big issue that bitcoin solves is security. According to a study done by LexisNexis, the United States alone sees about $190 billion dollars in credit card fraud each year. [viii]

The statistics on credit card fraud and data breaches are staggering. Even with the transition to the new EMV credit cards with the chip, theft from fraud and data breaches are still on the rise. Facebook, Microsoft, Equifax, and Yahoo have all had data breaches in which millions of customers' information was stolen.

By using bitcoin, it's likely that we could eliminate a large part, if not all, of the costs of this kind of fraud. This is because by using bitcoin, you're not giving away any personal information at all. As long as you use a secure wallet and don't leave your bitcoins on an exchange, your funds are safe and you're not exposed to identity theft.

One of the main reasons we have credit cards in the first place is that there is an inherent lack of trust between two parties in any transaction. Let's say a merchant wants to sell something to a customer but doesn't know if the customer will pay or not. They can accept a check, but how will the merchant know that the check won't bounce? What credit cards do is allow merchants to know that they are being paid the full amount at the time of the purchase. By accepting credit cards, a merchant transfers the liability of their customer paying over to the credit card company.

But therein lies another problem: Now it's the credit card companies' job to prevent fraud and make sure the customer pays their debts. To do this, they need your identity. From your identity, they put together a profile of how risky you are as a borrower (i.e., your credit score). What this means is centralized companies holding onto your most personal information.

It's not just credit card companies that have your personal information; it's social networking sites, e-commerce sites, credit reporting sites, and more. The way cyber criminals commit credit card fraud is by stealing your identity and taking out a line of credit. If this happens, it can be a nightmare to take care of. But with bitcoin, there are no user accounts and your personal identity is not held by any centralized company.

In fact, you don't need to give away any information at all to use bitcoin. All you need to use bitcoin is a bitcoin wallet, which is quick and easy to set up. You don't need to give your email, phone number, name, or anything of the sort. Do keep in mind, though, that bitcoin is not anonymous; it's pseudonymous. This means that other people can see your public key and all the transactions along with it, but not who you actually are. If they really wanted to, they could potentially track your IP, but that's a conversation for another time. The important thing to note is that by using bitcoin, your identity is far out of the hands of cyber thieves.

You might wonder, *How does bitcoin create a system where identities are not needed and everyone can still trust each other?*

Again, it all has to do with the proof of work that the miners are doing. This is what makes bitcoin "trustless." When a merchant is paid in bitcoin, they know the transaction was valid and they now have possession of the funds. You can't fake a bitcoin transaction, because proof of work eliminates the double-spending problem. When a merchant sees that they have been paid in bitcoin, they know that they can follow through on their end of the agreement. They don't have to worry about the risk of chargebacks either, since all bitcoin transactions are irreversible. Merchants are able to eliminate the risk of not being paid at the same time as their customers are able to eliminate the risk of their identity being stolen. It's a win-win for both parties.

However, this doesn't mean that using bitcoin is scam-proof. Since bitcoin is so hard to trace and transactions are irreversible, it has made bitcoin a target for scammers. If someone you don't know is asking for you to pay in bitcoin, be *extremely* careful. Once you hit "send," there's no going back.

Another great thing about bitcoin is that there is no single point of failure. Most websites today are run on centralized servers. This makes them vulnerable to things like DDOS attacks and hacks. With the blockchain, the ledger is held as a copy on over a 100,000 computers across the world. You would have to take down at least 51 percent of the computers on the network to affect bitcoin, which at this point is essentially impossible.

The bitcoin network is around several thousand times more powerful than the top 500 supercomputers in the world combined. In its more than ten years of existence, no one has been able to hack it. The guy who almost "broke the internet" in 2008, Dan Kaminsky, tried to hack bitcoin in 2013 and failed. Others have tried, too, and all of them have failed.

Bitcoin was designed to be "antifragile"—a word Nicholas Nassim Taleb likes to use. Something that is antifragile will "benefit from shocks. [It will] thrive and grow when exposed to volatility, randomness, disorder, and stressors and love adventure, risk, and uncertainty" (Antifragile: Things That Gain from Disorder, 2012).

Bitcoin is a great example of something that is antifragile. It has only gotten stronger with its continued use.

Faster and More Cost-Effective Way of Transferring Money

Speed isn't an issue for credit card transactions, but for any transaction dealing with a bank, it is. You're probably used to seeing the words "two to three business days" anytime you transfer funds from one bank to another. You can order something on Amazon Prime and have it delivered to your door at around the same time the funds are settled with your bank transfer.

Moving money is just about transferring bits of data over the internet. Banks take longer to do this because they have very high compliance costs. With millions of transactions being processed per day, they need time to detect fraudulent transactions. Plus, they don't mind holding onto your money a little longer either. Bitcoin is trustless, so there are no compliance costs. There is no need for an intermediary to make sure the system is fair; it is already fair by default.

In addition, the banking infrastructure in the Unites States is slow and outdated. Most of the banks are using transaction-processing systems that are coded with a programming language invented in the 1950s. If you try to send money through a bank on a Friday after 5:00 p.m., you'll have to wait until Monday for the bank to process the transaction.

Bitcoin has built its own banking infrastructure, one that

doesn't rely on the banks. The bitcoin ledger is updated about every ten minutes and the miners are working 24/7 to process transactions. Each transaction usually takes three confirmations and is settled in about thirty minutes or less. There are no weekends, business hours, or holidays on the blockchain. Bitcoin is on all the time.

Another area bitcoin could play a major role is by saving merchants on fees. Merchants pay out a percentage of every transaction to credit card companies and payment processors. On top of that, they have to pay upfront costs for the hardware and ongoing monthly fees. Companies like MasterCard, Visa, Stripe, and PayPal all have to make money. They have to pay for office space, salaries of employees, and expensive executives. These costs get passed on to the merchants which ultimately gets reflected in the prices of the goods and services we consume. If accepting payments was free, merchants would be able to lower their prices.

The great thing about bitcoin is that the fees for transferring money are a great deal less than accepting payment through traditional methods. The transactions are processed by miners, who take only a few cents to process the transaction and record it onto the blockchain. For the first time in history, you can move millions of dollars anywhere in the world for less than $1.

The Bitcoin Effect

Here are some of the results of what would happen if bitcoin started to gain mass adoption:

Billions of People Will Gain Access to Banking.

Still today, there are about 1.7 billion adults who don't have a bank account.[ix] The primary reasons include lack of money, an absence of trusted institutions, fees, and the distance from a bank. With bitcoin, anyone with a smartphone can be their own bank. It's that simple. All you need is a bitcoin wallet, and there are several good ones to choose from on the IOS and Android app stores. Even the new Samsung Galaxy S10 will have a built-in wallet for storing cryptocurrencies.

However, it's not just about giving people a bank account and a way to transfer money; it's actually much bigger than that. It's about giving people access to the tools they need to allow them to participate in financial markets. This means people in disadvantaged countries can begin to see their businesses grow, their capital appreciate, and their wealth preserved. Bitcoin and blockchain technology will likely be the largest wealth transfer in history, greater than both the Industrial Revolution and the Dot-Com Boom. The wealth of previous booms was mostly captured by people in developed countries that already had money. What bitcoin and blockchain will do is make it possible for anyone to participate in these financial markets.

This could mean a line of credit for a farmer in Argentina so they can take out a loan on a new property. Or it could mean someone in Indonesia investing in the S&P 500 index and matching the top investors on Wall St.

If you already own bitcoin, you can use it as collateral to take out a loan. This means that you can hold onto your bitcoin while you take out a loan to start a business. This is all done using the blockchain, making it fast and transparent. With the blockchain, you can apply and receive approval for a loan in a matter of minutes. The days of paying processing fees, origination fees, and waiting forever for a loan approval are going away.

Another good example of this is a company named Abra (http://www.abra.com) that is rolling out a feature to allow users purchase stocks and ETFs with bitcoin. Again, this means access to financial markets for those who need it most.

Cross-Border Payments Will Be Easier, Faster, and Cheaper than Ever.

If you've ever sent money overseas to a friend or relative, you know that it's a painful process. Not only is it inconvenient, it's also costly. When you send money overseas, you pay for it in two ways: exchange rates and fees. If you send money from US dollars to Euros and the current exchange rate is $1 equals €0.88, you won't get that. The recipient might only get €0.80 for every dollar you send. On top of that, you'll have to pay fees for each transaction.

On average, sending money overseas will cost you a little over 7 percent if you use a money transfer service and about 10 percent if you go through a bank.

The process is also painfully slow. The person receiving the money may have to wait as many as five days for the funds to settle. With bitcoin, it's nearly instant and nearly free. A bitcoin is a bitcoin no matter where you are in the world. Sending bitcoin is similar to sending an email or a message on WhatsApp. It doesn't matter where you are in the world; as long as you have an internet connection, you can send bitcoin. By using bitcoin, you don't have to deal with banks, physical locations, high fees, or someone rejecting your transaction.

One great example of this is one that Neil Patel, the digital marketer and author, gave about how he used bitcoin for his business. Neil was going to a conference in Asia that was paying him over $50,000 to come and speak. They had the money in the bank account, but it would have taken them over a month to send Neil the money. They had already tried a couple of times, but it didn't go through. With bitcoin, they were able to send him the money almost instantly. According to Neil, bitcoin is a way to send money "without having to deal with all this bureaucracy and banks."[x]

Each year, about $700 billion is sent overseas in the form of remittances alone. [xi] Assuming that we can save 5 percent in transaction costs by using bitcoin, that would mean a savings of $35 billion per year.

Corrupt Governments Will No Longer Be Able to

Place Strict Banking Controls on Their Citizens.

Being your own bank account is now as easy as owning a smartphone. Because of this, it will become increasingly difficult for governments to place tight banking controls on their citizens.

In 2017, 3.3 billion people lived under a dictatorship.[xii] Moreover, only 4.5 percent of the world lived in a fully functioning democracy.[xiii] Bitcoin is a way to push back against the corrupt governments that steal everything from their citizens and squander their wealth.

It will be nearly impossible for a country to shut down bitcoin. The only way they could shut down bitcoin is by shutting off the internet. Eventually, that won't even work with some of the new developments in the bitcoin technology. They can try to shut down the exchanges but getting past that would be as easy as using a virtual private network (VPN) or a decentralized exchange. Governments will have no choice but to allow their citizens to use bitcoin, giving them more freedom than ever before.

Here is what just a few of the smartest, most respected

people in the world think about bitcoin:

- **Elon Musk***:* "Paper money is going away, and crypto is a far better way to transfer value than pieces of paper, that's for sure." He also said, "Bitcoin is genius."[xiv]
- **Bill Gates**: "Bitcoin is exciting because it shows how cheap it can be. Bitcoin is better than currency in that you don't have to be physically in the same place and, of course, for large transactions, currency can get pretty inconvenient."[xv]

- **Richard Branson**: "I have invested in Bitcoin because I believe in its potential, the capacity it has to transform global payments is very exciting."[xvi]

- **Jack Dorsey,** founder and CEO of Twitter and Square Cash: "The world ultimately will have a single currency, [and] the internet will have a single currency. I personally believe that it will be bitcoin." [xvii]
- **Steve Wozniak,** Co-founder of Apple: "What an

incredible thing bitcoin is. Nobody runs it and owns it and yet it works so well." [xviii]

Chapter 3

How to Use Bitcoin

Now that you understand what bitcoin is and why it is important, you're probably wondering how you can actually use it.

All cryptocurrencies work the same way. For that reason, I will sometimes refer to cryptocurrencies as a whole, rather than just saying "bitcoin." Also note that "crypto" is just short for "cryptocurrency" and the word "coins" just refers to the cryptocurrencies as well.

The most important concepts in understanding how cryptocurrencies work is knowing how they are sent and received. To understand that, you will need to know what public and private keys are and how they work. We'll get to that in just a minute, but first let's take a look at the two places where cryptocurrencies can be sent and received from.

Wallets and Exchanges

Wallets

A wallet is a place where you will store your cryptocurrencies. It's similar to your physical wallet in your pocket, only it exists in the digital sense. The more complicated definition is a software program that stores your public and private keys. (Again, we'll get into public and private keys in just a minute)

A wallet will allow you to send and receive cryptocurrencies as well as manage your funds. You will need a wallet to safely store cryptocurrency. There are different types of wallets with varying levels of security, which we will also cover in just a bit.

Exchanges

An exchange is where you will first buy cryptocurrencies with dollars. You can also use an exchange to trade cryptocurrencies for one another. So, let's say you bought a bitcoin and would like to exchange it for ethereum, another popular cryptocurrency. You may need to use an exchange to do so. However, many wallets nowadays will let you do this directly from within the wallet, but not all. Using a cryptocurrency exchange is not all that different from using a stock exchange.

In the early days, obtaining a bitcoin was not the easiest thing to do. There weren't nearly as many exchanges available as there are today. In the very early days, you had to mine bitcoin on your computer, get it from a "faucet," or have someone sell it to you directly. It wasn't easy for the average person.

As bitcoin has become more mainstream, more exchanges have come about. Buying cryptocurrencies is now easier than ever before. For most of the major cryptocurrencies, all you will need is a smartphone and a credit or debit card. However, buying cryptocurrencies is just one step in a two-part process. After you've bought crypto, the next step becomes securing your coins. This extra step is necessary because of the way crypto is decentralized.

When you create an account on Google, all of the other apps are linked to that account. You can access Gmail, YouTube, and Google Drive all from the email and password you set. The same is true for Amazon. You can access Amazon Prime, Amazon Music, and Amazon Prime Video all from the same account. The same is true of stock exchanges. When you open up a brokerage account, you just set an email and password and can start trading.

With bitcoin, there are no user accounts. This means that, although crypto exchanges may look like stock exchanges, they have a key distinction that separates them: What happens after you purchase crypto is entirely different than what happens after you purchase stocks.

When you want to buy shares of stock in a company, you purchase that stock through the exchange. When you're ready to sell your stock, you just log into your account and hit "sell." There's no need to ever take your shares of stock off the exchange.

With crypto, it is the exact opposite. You *want* to take your cryptos off the exchange as quickly as possible and store them in a secure wallet (unless you are day-trading). When you leave your crypto on an exchange, you don't really own your crypto; the exchange does. Most crypto exchanges are centralized and unregulated, making them vulnerable to hacks and theft. Crypto wallets, on the other hand, are decentralized. This means they give you your private keys, which places you in full control of your crypto.

It's helpful to think of crypto wallets not as a company, but rather as a technology. They are just a tool that you use to use to interact with the blockchain to send and receive crypto. All you need to interact with the blockchain is a public and private key. What wallets do is store those keys in a user interface that makes it easy for you to use.

The important thing to keep in mind is that it is entirely your responsibility to secure your crypto assets. There is no insurance if they are lost or stolen. The decentralized nature of cryptocurrencies is what makes them so secure, trustless, and transparent. However, it also means there are more steps involved in securing your crypto assets. This is the cost of decentralization.

Also keep in mind that not all wallets and exchanges are created equally. Some exchanges such as Coinbase have done a great job of securing your crypto for you. Coinbase even has their own insurance policy to protect you if they are hacked. But many other exchanges I would never trust leaving my crypto in.

Public and Private Keys

Cryptocurrencies are sent from one person to another using wallets and exchanges. If you remember from the title of Satoshi's paper, it is a "peer-to-peer electronic cash" system. When you send crypto, it's going directly from your wallet or exchange to someone else's wallet or exchange. This is unlike traditional methods of sending money. Traditionally, when you send money to someone, it has to go from one banking institution to another before it ends up in the hands of the recipient.

Again, an important thing to keep in mind is that crypto transactions are not reversible. Once you send your crypto, that's it. There's no going back.

Unlike a credit card company, you cannot call a crypto company and say, "I sent my money to the wrong person Can you reverse the transaction?" There is no such number to call. This is why it's a good idea to send small amounts when you're first getting started to make sure you get the hang of it.

Cryptocurrencies are sent using public and private keys.

Understanding public and private keys is the most important part in understanding how all cryptocurrencies work.

Both wallets and exchanges will have public and private keys. But with exchanges, you only have access to your public keys and they hold the private keys for you.

Public and private keys are a long string of random numbers and letters. They are used to create what's called the "cryptographic functions" (also called "asymmetric cryptography")—hence, the term "crypto" in *crypto*currencies.

It sounds complicated, but it's actually a pretty simple concept.

Think of it this way: There are a bunch of P.O. boxes in a room and you want to leave some money in an envelope for a friend. Your friend told you that the P.O. box that belongs to him has the lettering "B12." This is his "public key."

Knowing this public key allows you to locate the box so you can place the envelope in the small slip.

When your friend comes back to pick up the money, he will need to use his physical key to unlock the P.O. box and access the envelope. His physical key is his "private key." His private key is unique to that P.O. box and cannot be used to open any other P.O. box other than B12.

As the person depositing the envelope, you do not have access to what's inside the P.O. box because you don't have the physical key. You only know the public key to be able to locate the box. This means you can only place the envelope in the box but cannot retrieve it once it's there.

Public and private keys work the same way with cryptocurrencies. The public key is used to direct where you want to send the money to and the private key is used to access the funds.

However, with cryptocurrencies, there are two more things to keep in mind: the passcode to your wallet and the backup phrase. For that reason, I'll make this analogy to a bank account:

- **Public Key** (aka public address): This is like the routing number for your bank account. Again, it is the address people will need to have if they want to send you money.
- **Private Key**: This is like the authentication code you need for your bank to verify that it was actually you who initiated the transaction (i.e., two-factor authentication).
- **Passcode**: This is like the log-in credentials you need to access your bank account (i.e., username and password).
- **Backup Phrase**: This is like the security questions to identify that it is really you in case you get locked out of your bank account.

Let me elaborate on that a little …

Public Key or Public Address

Your public key is like your routing number to your bank account. It's what people will use to send money to directly to your bank. You don't want to go around telling everyone your public key to your wallet, but it's not nearly as sensitive as your private key.

You could also make the analogy to your email address. Again, don't go giving it out to strangers, but you do need to give it to people if you want them to send you an email you.

Most crypto wallets also use QR codes. This allows you to scan a wallet's public key so you don't have to copy and paste that long string of letters and numbers. It's a simple, yet powerful technology that makes cryptocurrency even easier to send. If you are sending to a public key without using a QR code, you simply copy and paste the public key.

Your public key will look something like this:

"1MZjmvTSkrDKCWfcCkNhRtCerrN9nEYTgp"

Just keep in mind that putting in the wrong public key or scanning the wrong QR code will result in your crypto going to the wrong person.

Private Keys

Image if every time you initiated a transaction through

your bank, the bank would send you an email or a text with a unique code. You would then have to input that code back into the website of your bank where you initiated the transaction. This is what we would call "two-factor authentication" (2FA), and the intention is to verify that it really is you who wants to send money.

With bitcoin, the private key is used to "sign" each transaction leaving your wallet to ensure that it was you who wants to send the money. Just like the key to the P.O. box corresponds to only that specific box, the same is true for cryptocurrencies. Each private keys corresponds to one public key.

The good news is that you don't ever have to see your private key or even know what it is. It is encrypted onto the device that you have the wallet on. It's there to sign every transaction leaving your wallet, telling the bitcoin network that the transaction did, in fact, come from you. The private key works in the background. As long as you are using a wallet from your own phone or laptop, you shouldn't have to input, write down, or remember your private key at all. Only when you import your wallet to another wallet will you have to deal with this. It's best to leave the private keys alone and not export them anywhere.

Passcode

The passcode to your wallet is like the log-in credentials to your bank account. Just like the private key, it is what gives you permission you to access your funds. Since the private key is being stored on the device, all a hacker would need is your passcode if they had your device in hand. (There are ways to prevent this with multi-sig wallets.)

The passcode in a crypto wallet is just like the passcode to sign into your smartphone or laptop. Some crypto wallets will ask you to make a four or six-digit pin. Others will let you create your own custom password or use the fingerprint ID you have set up on your smartphone. The passcode is what keeps intruders out of your wallet, but beyond that, it won't restore your wallet if you lose your device or it gets wiped. For obvious reasons, it's important to set a passcode that is both difficult to guess and easy for you to remember. Don't just use "1111."

Backup Passphrase (aka mnemonic phrase, seed

phrase, or master seed)

Your backup passphrase is *extremely important!* In fact, it is the most important part of the entire crypto wallet. This is what you will need to keep written down and stored somewhere safe and not let anyone find out. Unlike a simple four-digit passcode, it is hard to remember and very easy to lose.

The purpose behind the backup phrase is to recover your wallet in case you lose access to it somehow. Say you lose your phone, your laptop, or your hardware wallet. You can still recover your funds if you saved the backup passphrase. There are plenty of stories of people who lost a great deal of money in crypto because they lost their backup phrase. Don't be that person.

Your backup phrase will be twelve or twenty-four random words.

Make sure you write it down, make a copy, and laminate it so it's waterproof. Some people put it in a fireproof safe or keep it in a safety deposit box. Take out a pen and paper and physically write it down; don't just take a screenshot of the backup phrase.

Also, it's best not to type the backup phrase on any device that's connected to the internet. However, I break this rule a little with LastPass. What I personally do is write down my backup phrase physically on a piece of paper and laminate it so it doesn't get ruined. Then I back up that by typing the phrase into LastPass. I trust LastPass because they have 256-bit encryption, and their whole business model is centered around keeping their customer data safe.

This is something you probably won't hear from other people, but honestly, I'm more afraid of losing my backup phrase by keeping it on one piece of paper than I am about LastPass getting hacked. Just make sure the device you're using is secure and doesn't have any malware.

No matter what kind of wallet you have, as long as you have that backup passphrase, you can always restore your wallet and get your crypto back.

Before You Buy Any Bitcoin...

Here are a few things to keep in mind before you buy any amount of bitcoin:

It's a high-risk investment.

There's no such thing as a sure investment. Every investment has risk, and every good investor knows that past performance does not guarantee future results. Even though the blockchain is widely accepted as a promising technology, the future of bitcoin is still uncertain. This is the case for two reasons.

The first is that it's too early to tell if bitcoin will become mainstream or not. There's a lot of vested interest in the dollar. Even though governments can't stop bitcoin, they can do some things to deter people from using it. There are also still some barriers to entry that keep people from adopting bitcoin. The prices of bitcoin is highly volatile. This results in many people speculating on the prices, rather than use them it as a currency the way it was intended to be.

The second reason to consider is that even if cryptocurrencies do become mainstream, we don't know which ones will be the winners. Bitcoin was the first and has a huge head start, but that doesn't mean that will always be the case. Bitcoin still has some issues with scaling that could present an opportunity for another cryptocurrency to come in and take its place.

It's also not clear yet if cryptocurrencies are a zero-sum game. That is to say, there may be several cryptocurrencies for each niche, or they may all go to zero except for a handful. By investing in cryptocurrencies, you're first betting that cryptocurrencies will become mainstream, then your betting that you know the ones that will succeed. It's not an easy investment. Investing in cryptocurrencies today is similar to investing in internet companies in the 1990s: Most people were not able to predict that the internet would take off the way it did, let alone be able to pick the handful of companies that control most of the market share today (Google, Amazon, Facebook, etc.).

There's a lot of volatility.

Another thing to keep in mind is that cryptocurrencies tend to be volatile. If you believe in it for the long term, this shouldn't scare you away. However, don't be surprised if you see your investment loses 50 percent of its value in a week, or more.

Here are a few basic rules for crypto investing:

- **Don't invest more than you can afford to lose**. Seriously. This is the most important rule to investing in bitcoin and other cryptocurrencies and I'm still surprised at how many people don't follow this rule. Don't bet on cryptocurrencies being your key to obtaining wealth beyond your wildest imagination. I get it: It's fun to fantasize what life would be like if you had bought bitcoin in 2012. It's the same reason why so many people play the lottery. But be extremely careful to not invest more than you can afford to lose. To help enforce this, you have to pretend like your money is already gone. You can't get emotionally attached to any amount of money you have in cryptocurrencies. Additionally, you should only invest a small percentage of your overall portfolio into cryptocurrencies if you decide to invest at all. (By portfolio, I mean you're the sum of all of your investments combined.) You may feel safe putting

2–3 percent of your portfolio in crypto—maybe 5 percent if you feel really good about it—but not more than that.

- **Don't get FOMO**. "FOMO" stands for "fear of missing out." FOMO is what created the bubble in 2017. Everyone was buying in because they were afraid they were going to miss out. It's important to know what price levels you feel comfortable investing in and be willing to walk away if the price is too high. If you are the type of person who will get FOMO and panic into investing, you're better off not investing at all.

- **Know your price.** With stocks, we can run different calculations to try to estimate if a stock is over or undervalued. With bitcoin, it's a bit different. Bitcoin doesn't really have an "intrinsic" value. Instead, it trades more based on technicals. It's ok if you are not an expert in technical analysis, however, it is helpful to have a basic understanding of bitcoin's price movements to make decisions on when and if to buy.

- **Don't invest in anything you don't understand.** This is one Warren Buffett is famous for saying and he's absolutely right. To use bitcoin, you don't need to know or care about the blockchain. If you just want to play around with some bitcoin with the spare cash you have, that's perfectly fine. But if you are investing in a cryptocurrency for a particular reason, then it is important to understand the underlying technology.

- **Know your tax obligations**. This is an important step before you invest in anything. You should always know exactly how you will be taxed as it will affect your investment strategy or your decision to invest at all. Your tax obligations for cryptocurrencies will vary depending on where you live. Please consult with a certified public accountant (CPA) for this.

- **Make sure it's legal to buy where you live**. Buying bitcoin in most places around the world is perfectly legal as long as you pay your taxes. However, do make sure to double-check since some countries have but temporary bans on its use.

- **Don't fall for the low prices**. Just because a cryptocurrency has a low price does not make it a good investment. Some people get scared away by the high price of bitcoin and instead invest in smaller cryptocurrencies. Most of these smaller cryptocurrencies will not be a good investment long term.

- **Keep your crypto safe**. Once you've invested in crypto, you will need to secure your coins by putting them in what's called a cold wallet. As I mentioned earlier, you do not want to leave your cryptos on the exchange, as they are vulnerable to theft. I prefer to use a hardware wallet such as the Ledger Nano S for cold storage. If you're actively day-trading crypto, then you will have to leave some amount of money on the exchange. Just remember not to keep all your funds on one exchange.

Buying Bitcoin

As you already know, you will need to use an exchange to buy bitcoin. There are a few wallets that allow you to buy bitcoin directly from within the wallet, but I would recommend using a traditional exchange so you can buy with lower fees, then move the bitcoin to a wallet after purchasing.

When it comes to exchanges, there are two companies that are dominant in the industry: Coinbase and Binance. In 2017, these two exchanges could not have been more opposite. Coinbase is based in the United States, so it is regulated and does everything by the book. It reports to the IRS and is registered as a money services business. Because of this, it has been much more selective about what cryptocurrencies it offers to buy and sell on its exchange. The advantage to using Coinbase is that it makes the process of buying cryptocurrencies extremely easy.

Binance, on the other hand, has put more of an emphasis on offering as many cryptocurrencies to buy and sell, and not as much of an emphasis on dealing with regulation.

Binance didn't even accept fiat currency until 2019. Before then, you would have to deposit bitcoin to Binance to use the exchange. What people would do is buy bitcoin from Coinbase and then transfer it over to Binance to trade it for another cryptocurrency.

Nowadays, these two exchanges look more similar to each other than they did before. Binance now offers its customers a way to buy bitcoin, ethereum, litecoin, and ripple with fiat currency. Coinbase has since added more cryptocurrencies, such as ripple and basic attention token to its exchange as well.

These two exchanges have been competing for users over the past few years, but in my opinion, they still serve two different roles. Coinbase is great for people who are new to crypto and just want to buy one of the most popular coins, such as bitcoin or ethereum. However, I would recommend you use Coinbase Pro instead of Coinbase. It is slightly more complicated, but you will save yourself a good amount in fees. The downside is you won't be able to buy with a credit or debit card, which means you will have to wait several days to deposit funds from your bank account.

Binance is great for more advanced users who want to trade cryptocurrencies or buy smaller altcoins. They have a powerful trading platform and now offer the ability to buy crypto with a credit or debit card. However, Binance is a bit more complicated to use than Coinbase and about the same as Coinbase Pro. Binance is defiantly your best option to buy any of the smaller cryptocurrencies if you already own some bitcoin or ethereum. You can easily deposit just about any crypto you want and exchange them for another with minimal fees.

The Best Method of Buying Crypto

I know it can be overwhelming to pick what products to use. For that reason, I've put together what I believe is the best setup for the majority of people. So here it is:

1. Deposit your funds via a bank account transfer to Coinbase Pro. (It will take several days to receive your funds.)
2. Once your funds arrive, place a market or limit order for the cryptocurrency you want. The difference in fees won't be much, so if you like the current market price, you can just place a market order.

3. If you don't want to buy any other cryptocurrencies, then you should transfer the crypto you bought to a wallet. If you've purchased more bitcoin in the dollar value than you would keep in your physical wallet, make sure you use a cold wallet such as the Ledger Nano S as that is the most secure.

4. If you do want to buy a smaller cryptocurrency that's not on Binance, you will need to send one of the cryptos you purchased off Coinbase Pro over to Binance. From there, you can trade just about any cryptocurrency pair you wish.

5. Next, you will need to pick a wallet to store your crypto unless you plan on actively trading them. Again, pick a secure cold wallet if you are investing any significant amount of money.

This is the best method because it is a cost effective and covers all your bases.

Safely Storing Your Bitcoin

By now, you know that you need a wallet to safely store bitcoin, but it's also important to know what kind of wallet you should use.

For storing small amounts of cryptocurrency, you can use what's called a "hot wallet," also called a "software wallet." A hot wallet is any wallet that is connected to the internet. Because it's connected to the internet, it makes your crypto easily accessible but also less secure. It's important to remember not to keep more money in a hot wallet than you would keep in your physical wallet. Hot wallets are more secure than exchanges, but they are by no means a full-proof way of storing large amounts of crypto.

The two most common types of hot wallets are mobile wallets and desktop wallets. The user interface for hot wallets will be more familiar to you. If you can use an app on a smartphone, you can use a hot wallet.

Setting Up Your Hot Wallet

Some wallets will ask for your email and for you to set a password to begin. If not, you will be asked if you want to "set up a new wallet" or "restore from backup." I prefer to use wallets that do not ask for my email. Even though signing up with your email might seem more familiar to you, it's helpful to get in the habit of not having to use your email. Remember, crypto is about giving you full custody of your funds, and you don't need to give away your identity to use bitcoin.

Since you are setting up a wallet for the first time, hit "set up a new wallet." You will then be asked to set a pin or a passcode to protect your wallet. This is for your device only and is to protect you in case someone steals your phone. It will not help you recover your bitcoin if your phone is wiped.

This next step is very important: You will now be prompted to back up your wallet. Some wallets let you skip this, but I would strongly recommend you go ahead and back it up. The wallet will give you a twelve-word phrase. Now is the time to get out a pen and paper and physically write it down. Don't just take a screenshot. Not only is taking a screenshot in an insecure way to store your backup phrase, in the next step you'll have to repeat the phrase back to them. Again, the backup phrase is what you will use to recover your wallet if anything happens.

Now you're off to the races. You have your wallet set up, and you can send and receive bitcoin. You can simply receive bitcoin by hitting the "receive" button and what you'll see is that it gives you an address to send the bitcoin to.

For storing larger amounts of bitcoin, you'll definitely want to use what's called a "cold wallet." Cold wallets are much more secure than hot wallets since they are not connected to the internet at all. The two types of cold wallets are paper wallets and hardware wallets.
The downside to using cold wallets is that they can be more difficult and inconvenient to use than hot wallets.

It's strongly recommended that, as a beginner, you don't use a paper wallet. This is because with paper wallets, it can be easy to accidently expose your private keys. It is also much more difficult to withdraw bitcoin from a paper wallet than any other kind of wallet.

Hardware wallets are, as you might have inferred from the name, a piece of hardware that stores your private keys. They are small enough to fit in your pocket, so you can carry it with you wherever you go. When you want to send bitcoin to someone, you'll just need to plug the device into a computer and use the interface that will pop up. Thankfully, it doesn't matter if you use a computer that has malware on it; the device will still be safe. In addition, you don't have to plug the device into a computer to receive bitcoin, only to send it. My personal favorite is the Ledger Nano S. It's secure, easy to use, and relatively affordable at around $50 on Amazon. However, you can also use the Trezor, which is an equally good hardware wallet as well.

Spending Bitcoin

Your reason for buying bitcoin may be to hold onto it as an investment for the long term. Or maybe you're going to day-trade and take advantage of the volatility. Maybe you live in a country with a weak national currency, and you want to hedge some of the risks.

Whatever your reason for owning bitcoin, one of the greatest things about it is that it is real money. It's not some make-believe internet money; it is a real currency that you can use to pay for just about anything.

What's even better is that you don't have to change the way you would normally pay for things. There are a few companies that allow you to keep your bitcoin on an account that's linked to a debit card. When you are ready to spend the bitcoin, you just swipe the card and it instantly converts to cash to pay for your items. The two most notable cards are Coinbase's Shift card and the BitPay card. You can also download an app to manage your balance, as well as withdraw cash from ATMs. Do keep in mind that there is an initial issuance fee for the cards that is about $15.

If you don't want to use a card to spend bitcoin, you can

still send bitcoin to anyone as long as you have their public address. You simply copy and paste their public address or scan their QR code to your wallet. You can also use spendabit.co or spendbitcoins.com to search for stores that accept bitcoin.

Accepting Bitcoin as a Business

If you own a business and want to accept bitcoin, it can easily be done. If you have a physical storefront, you can print out the QR code that is your public address. You can then laminate the QR code and have it displayed at your storefront. People will then scan the QR code with their wallet and send you the bitcoin. You don't have to worry about not receiving the bitcoin right away, because you can verify that the customer has sent it. You can go to a bitcoin block explorer and type in your public address, and you will see that a transaction is on the way (https://www.blockchain.com/explorer).

You can also rest assured that the customer will not be able to reverse the transaction, as bitcoin transactions are irreversible.

The downside to this option is that you will need to make sure that the customer is paying the correct amount in bitcoin. So, say bitcoin is at $5,000 and you're selling a pizza for $20. You will take $20 and divide it by $5,000 to get 0.004. You will need to charge them 0.004 bitcoin for the pizza, but what if they only send 0.003 to the QR code? You will need to have them show you how much bitcoin they sent by showing you their wallet or by going to the block explorer. Another downside to this option is that, by the time you receive the bitcoin, the price will be different. Most likely the price will only be slightly different and won't affect you, but sometimes, it's not so slight.

If you do decide to use this option, make sure you use a wallet that lets you instantly convert the bitcoin to cash. One example of a wallet that does this is Abra.

If that seems like too much work and you just want a turnkey solution, you can use a company like BitPay or Coinbase Commerce. These companies allow you to accept bitcoin by installing a payment button on your website, send crypto invoices via email, or accept bitcoin with a smartphone or tablet using their app. The great thing about this option is that it allows you to lock in the exchange rate, so you won't be faced with any price risk at all. The price you charge is the amount you get, minus their fees. This option is great for people who want to broaden their customer base by accepting bitcoin but have no interest in actually dealing with the bitcoin themselves. Just be aware that there is a 1 percent fee for using these services. However, this is still cheaper than accepting credit cards in many cases.

Final Thoughts

Congratulations! By now, you are an expert in bitcoin, compared to 99 percent of the rest of the world. You know how to buy, store, spend, and send crypto. You know what bitcoin is, how it works, and why it was created. You know why it's a technological breakthrough and how it can impact our society.

Chances are that when you are reading this, it will still be too early to tell what bitcoin's true impact will be. It will likely take a decade or more to find out. As a comparison, I would say that bitcoin in 2019 is about at the same stage as the internet was in 1998.

In many ways, this industry is evolving very similar to the way the internet did: There was the initial hype, skepticism, an over-investment, and a resulting bubble that eventually burst. In the end, a handful of companies emerged that changed the world forever.

Everything in crypto has followed the same trajectory, except for the last part. We don't yet know who the main players in the crypto industry will be. But what we do know is this: crypto and blockchain aren't going away anytime soon. There has only been an increase in activity from companies and government all over the world. From JP Morgan to Dubai to Facebook, we will see billions of dollars invested in this space in the coming years.

Understanding how Bitcoin works will only be to your advantage. Whether you're an entrepreneur, an executive, or a lawyer, the blockchain will impact how you do business. You don't have to own any bitcoin or write code, but knowing what it is and how it works will only become more important as time goes on.

It is my belief that bitcoin and blockchain will ultimately be used as a force for good in the world. Disrupting technologies always seem scary. Many people are afraid that artificial intelligence could replace humans. While that concern is warranted, AI can also be used for uncovering cures for cancer and many other beneficial applications. There's always a yin and a yang to new technology. Some people will use it for good; some people will exploit it for their own benefit. The technology itself is agnostic. It is the humans who use it that shape whether it is good or bad.

The same was true of the internet. Many of the early uses of the internet were for criminal activities. However, today, we use the internet on a daily basis to stay connected with our friends and family and most of us couldn't imagine a life without it.

The internet is about connecting people to let them communicate with one another. The blockchain is about connecting people to let them trust one another. The internet is a tool for communication, while the blockchain is a tool for trust. What we will likely see over the next couple of years is that more people will adopt bitcoin and blockchain for its benefits, not for its hype. Businesses will do it to increase efficiency and cut costs. People will do it because they will now have more power in the systems that govern them, and they, too, will receive an economic benefit. The future for bitcoin and blockchain is exciting, but before you go, here are a few quick reminders:

1. Never invest more than you can afford to lose.
2. Don't keep bitcoin on an exchange, transfer it to a wallet.
3. Don't keep more money in your hot wallet than you

would keep cash in your actual physical wallet.

4. Use a hardware wallet to store bitcoin for the long term.

5. Backup your wallet by writing down the twelve- or twenty-four-word backup phrase and keep up in a safe place.

Reviews

If you enjoyed this book, it would be greatly appreciated if you could leave your thoughts on Amazon. Your positive review will help other readers find the book.

Feedback

We're always happy to hear your feedback! Email us at contact@cryptomavericks.io

JOSH MILLER AND MATT LOPEZ

About the Authors

Josh Miller

Hey there!

My name is Josh Miller and I want to quickly share a little bit about myself. Before I do, I want to say thank you for taking the time to educate yourself on bitcoin, crypto and the future economy. It means a lot to me.

My Background as an entrepreneur is in building systems, high-level finance, and cutting-edge marketing strategies.

In 2017, I Co-founded an influencer/full-scale Digital Marketing Agency named Invigor8 with several of my closest friends. With a lot of hard work and a little luck, we've had some great success.

I've also been heavily involved in Bitcoin since 2012 and in other cryptocurrencies soon thereafter.

I have now decided to shift my focus almost entirely to building in the blockchain and cryptocurrency space with my latest company, Crypto Mavericks.

Our Mission at Crypto Mavericks is simple: "To put the power of Blockchain technology into the hands of billions of people."

We will accomplish this ambitions mission by bringing together a collective mind and by educating individuals as well as empowering crypto companies with the right values.

Together, we will make this vision that we all have for a more fair, transparent, and prosperous society a reality, one day at a time.

Matthew Lopez

Matthew Lopez is an author, entrepreneur and lifelong learner. He has helped build multiple businesses from digital marketing to blockchain startups before the age of 22. He began his journey in the online world in 2015, learning everything he could about technology, marketing, and finance.

He soon became obsessed with the impact that bitcoin and blockchain technology will have on society. He has since given several presentations on the implications of this new technology and how it can be across various industries such as finance and real estate.

At his latest role the Co-founder of Crypto Mavericks, he oversees all of the content, influencer network, brand partnerships, and digital marketing.

References

[i] (BitcoinTalk, "How anonymous are bitcoins?" November 25, 2009).

[ii] Ingraham, Christopher. "The IRS Took Millions from Innocent People Because of How They Managed Their Bank Accounts, Inspector General Finds." The Washington Post. April 05, 2017. Accessed April 26, 2019. https://www.washingtonpost.com/news/wonk/wp/2017/04/05/the-irs-took-millions-from-innocent-people-because-of-how-they-managed-their-bank-accounts-inspector-general-finds/?noredirect=on.

[iii] (from the foreword to *The Bitcoin Standard: The Decentralized Alternative to Central Banking* by Saifedean Ammous).

[iv] in a speech on "Deflation: Making Sure 'It' Doesn't Happen Here"

[v] "Bitcoin P2P e-cash paper," November 8, 2008

[vi] HernÁndez, Carlos. "Bitcoin Has Saved My Family." The New York Times. February 23, 2019. Accessed April 26, 2019. https://www.nytimes.com/2019/02/23/opinion/sunday/venezuela-bitcoin-inflation-cryptocurrencies.html.

[vii] "Bitcoin open source implementation of P2P currency," February 11, 2009

[viii] Shaughnessy, Haydn. "Solving the $190 Billion Annual Fraud Problem: More on Jumio." Forbes. April 15, 2012. Accessed May 29, 2019.

https://www.forbes.com/sites/haydnshaughnessy/2011/03/24/solving-the-190-billion-annual-fraud-scam-more-on-jumio/.

[ix] "Home | Global Findex." Home | Global Findex. Accessed April 26, 2019. https://globalfindex.worldbank.org/.

[x] "Is Cryptocurrency REALLY Here to Stay?" YouTube video, 5:30, "Neil Patel," July 19, 2018, https://www.youtube.com/watch?v=eJJEQQFCQao

[xi] Tanzi, Alexandre. "Strong Advanced Economies Fuel Record 2018 Remittance Flows." Bloomberg.com. December 10, 2018. Accessed April 26, 2019. https://www.bloomberg.com/news/articles/2018-12-10/strong-advanced-economies-fuel-record-2018-remittance-flows.

[xii] "Ever More People Worldwide Living under Dictatorship, German Study Finds." The Local. March 22, 2018. Accessed April 26, 2019. https://www.thelocal.de/20180322/ever-more-people-worldwide-living-under-dictatorship-german-study-finds.

[xiii] Erickson, Amanda. "U.S. Democracy Is in Grave Danger, a New Economist Report Warns." The Washington Post. February 01, 2018. Accessed April 26, 2019. https://www.washingtonpost.com/news/worldviews/wp/2018/02/01/u-s-democracy-is-in-grave-danger-a-new-economist-report-warns/.

[xiv] Zhao, Wolfie. "Elon Musk Calls Bitcoin 'Brilliant,' Better Than Paper Money for Value Transfer." CoinDesk. February 20, 2019. Accessed April 26, 2019. https://www.coindesk.com/elon-musk-calls-bitcoin-brilliant-better-than-paper-money-for-value-transfer.

[xv] Elkins, Kathleen. "Bill Gates in 2014: Bitcoin Is 'better than Currency'." CNBC. December 19, 2017. Accessed April 26, 2019. https://www.cnbc.com/2017/12/19/bill-gates-in-2014-bitcoin-is-better-than-currency.html.

[xvi] "How Digital Currency Could Transform the World." Virgin. December 11, 2015. Accessed April 26, 2019. https://www.virgin.com/richard-branson/how-digital-currency-could-transform-the-world.

[xvii] Bambrough, Billy. "Twitter CEO Jack Dorsey Has Made A Bold Prediction About Bitcoin." Forbes. April 08, 2019. Accessed April 26, 2019. https://www.forbes.com/sites/billybambrough/2019/02/04/twitter-ceo-jack-dorsey-has-made-a-bold-prediction-about-bitcoin/.

[xviii] Cointelegraph. "Steve Wozniak: "What an Incredible Thing Bitcoin Is"." YouTube. June 05, 2018. Accessed April 26, 2019. https://www.youtube.com/watch?v=Z7apkWvlDxk.